Nelson Mandela

Copyright © 2015 by Quelle Histoire / quellehistoire.com
Published by Roaring Brook Press
Roaring Brook Press is a division of Holtzbrinck Publishing Holdings Limited Partnership
175 Fifth Avenue, New York, NY 10010
mackids.com

Library of Congress Control Number: 2017957518
ISBN 978-1-250-16613-5

Our books may be purchased in bulk for promotional, educational, or business use. Please contact your local bookseller or the Macmillan Corporate and Premium Sales Department at (800) 221-7945 ext. 5442 or by e-mail at MacmillanSpecialMarkets@macmillan.com.

First published in France in 2015 by Quelle Histoire, Paris
First U.S. edition, 2018

Text: Albin Quéru, Romain Jubert
Translation: Catherine Nolan
Illustrations: Bruno Wennagel, Mathieu Ferret, Guillaume Biasse

Printed in China by RR Donnelley Asia Printing Solutions Ltd., Dongguan City, Guangdong Province
10 9 8 7 6 5 4 3 2 1

Nelson Mandela

Roaring Brook Press
New York

Childhood

Nelson Mandela spent his life fighting injustice in South Africa. His triumph inspired people around the world. Nelson was born in 1918 in a village called Mvezo. His parents named him Rolihlahla. A teacher gave him the English name Nelson, and the name stuck.

1918

Apartheid

When Nelson was growing up, South Africa had a system called *apartheid*.

Under apartheid, white people had more rights than black people. White people ran the government. They told black people where they could live and what jobs they could have. They rarely let black people vote.

The system was cruel and unfair.

1918–1944

The Struggle

Nelson wanted to find a way to end apartheid. In 1944, he joined a group called the African National Congress. The group used peaceful protests to speak out against apartheid.

But the government refused to listen. In 1960, police opened fire on protestors, killing 69 people.

Nelson decided that peaceful protest wasn't enough. He created a new group called the Spear of the Nation. This group was armed and ready to use force if necessary.

———

1944–1961

Prison

Nelson was arrested for opposing the government. He was sentenced to life in prison.

Nelson's cell didn't have a bed or plumbing. He was allowed to receive only one letter every six months. And he was forced to do hard labor.

Still, Nelson kept fighting apartheid from his cell. He earned a law degree so he could argue against unjust laws. He organized protests with other prisoners. He wrote powerful political statements. Nelson's words helped convince people just how wrong apartheid was.

———

1962–1976

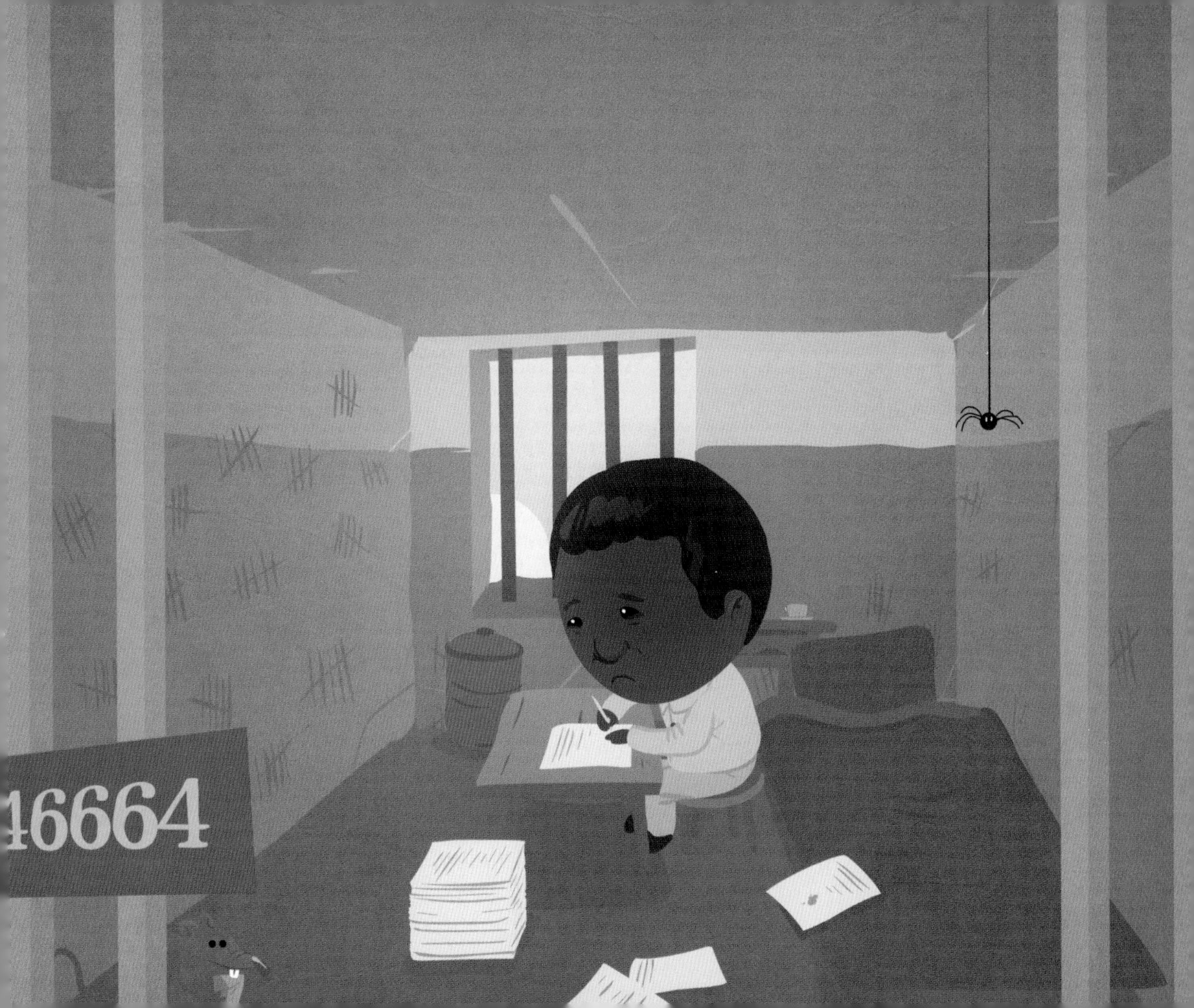
46664

Soweto

More and more South Africans joined the battle against apartheid.

In 1976, teachers and students held a huge protest in the city of Soweto. Violence broke out between the police and the protestors. Hundreds of demonstrators died.

Still, the protests continued. The South African government tried to make a deal with Nelson. If he would tell people to stop protesting apartheid, they would let him go. Nelson said no.

Nelson stayed in prison for twenty-seven years.

1976

Freedom

South Africa got a new president in 1989, Frederik de Klerk. He made a surprising announcement on February 2, 1990. He was going to free Nelson!

On February 11, 1990, Nelson finally left prison. He began working with Frederik. Together, they struck down their country's unfair laws and ended apartheid.

At last, black people and white people in South Africa had the same rights.

——

1989–1991

The Nobel Prize

Nelson and Frederik went to Norway in 1993 to receive a special award. It was the Nobel Peace Prize, awarded for their work ending apartheid and starting a new government.

People around the world admired Nelson. He stood for fairness and freedom, not only in South Africa, but everywhere.

———

1993

President

In 1994, Nelson ran for president of South Africa. It was the first time in the country that people of all races were allowed to vote.

Nelson cast his own vote in a small schoolhouse. "I have just voted for the first time in my life," he said joyfully.

Nelson won the election. On May 10, 1994, he was sworn in as the first black president of South Africa.

———

1994

World Cup

Nelson's job was not easy. Apartheid was over, but there were still hard feelings between black people and white people. Nelson had to find ways to bring everyone together.

In 1995, South Africa hosted the Rugby World Cup. Rugby had always been thought of as a sport for white people in South Africa. But Nelson urged every citizen to support the team . . . even if their chance of winning was pretty slim.

To everyone's shock, South Africa's team won the World Cup! People all over the country—both black and white—cheered. It was a step toward uniting the nation.

_____

1995

Rainbow Nation

Nelson never stopped working for justice and peace. He died on December 5, 2013. More than one hundred leaders from other countries made the trip to South Africa for his funeral, an event that touched the whole world.

___

2013

1914
First World War begins.

1927
Nelson's father dies.

1944
Nelson joins the African National Congress.

1900

1918
Nelson Mandela is born.

1939
Second World War begins.

1952
He starts the country's first black law firm.

1958
Nelson marries Winnie Madikizela.

1962
Nelson is sent to jail.

1990
Nelson is released from prison.

1994
Nelson is elected president.

2013
Nelson Mandela dies.

2014

1960
The African National Congress is banned by the government.

1976
Protests break out in Soweto.

1993
Nelson and Frederik win the Nobel Peace Prize.

1999
Nelson finishes his term as president.

NAMIBIA

BOTSWANA

MOZAMBIQUE

SOUTH
AFRICA

⑤

③

④

①

AFRICA

② ⑥

SOUTH AFRICA

Mvezo

Nelson was born and grew up in this small village in southeastern South Africa.

2 **Robben Island**

Nelson was imprisoned for eighteen of his twenty-seven-year sentence on this island. In 1997, the prison became a museum.

3 Johannesburg

Nelson started South Africa's first black law firm in this busy city.

4 Durban

This city was home to many people and groups who fought against apartheid.

5 Pretoria

Nelson was sworn in as president here in 1994.

6 Cape Town

Founded in 1652, this is one of the oldest cities in South Africa. It's near Robben Island, where Nelson was jailed.

People to Know

Desmond Tutu
(Born in 1931)
Desmond started off as a teacher
and later became a bishop. He helped
Nelson bring peace to South Africa
after apartheid ended. Desmond won
the Nobel Peace Prize in 1984.

Frederik de Klerk
(Born in 1936)
This politician released Nelson from
prison and worked with Nelson to end
apartheid.

Winnie Mandela
(Born in 1936)
Winnie, Nelson's second wife, worked
for justice alongside him. She led
protests of her own, too.

François Pienaar
(Born in 1967)
François was the captain of the rugby
team that won the 1995 World Cup.

....

In 1952, Nelson started the first black law firm in South Africa.

....

The political statements that Nelson wrote in prison were smuggled to the outside world. His words inspired others to oppose apartheid.

Like Nelson, Winnie Mandela was arrested and imprisoned for fighting apartheid.

Nelson came up with clever ways to communicate with other prisoners in jail. He hid notes in toilet tanks and under piles of dishes.

Available Now

 Muhammad Ali

 Neil Armstrong

 Blackbeard

 Coco Chanel

 Charlie Chaplin

Cleopatra

 Marie Curie

 Albert Einstein

 Abraham Lincoln

 Nelson Mandela

 Isaac Newton

 Rosa Parks

Coming Soon

 Anne Frank

 Gandhi

 Frida Kahlo

 Martin Luther King, Jr.